Dear Grandma

by
Marianne Richmond

To

From

Date

I love you,
grandma...

for being

wonderful
you.

I love your goodness.

And how
your smile
and laughter
warm a room.

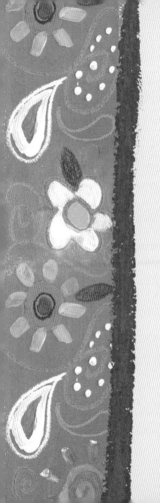

I love being around you.

*You make
your family
feel incredibly
special.*

I so appreciate
the kind things

Your
thoughtful
gifts and
caring words.

And, of course, your treats...

Those yummy expressions of love
that no one else can seem to
duplicate, no matter how
hard we try!

I value

your

perspective

and

life

experience.

I love listening to you
tell your stories

of growing up with

your kids.

And how you

gently share a

tidbit of

wisdom

that you know

might come in

handy for

me someday.

You provide this

wonderful connection

to days gone by that

I can never know.

I love that you're my grand-mom and not my mom-mom. You have patience and perspective and humor to spare.

And you can thankfully separate yourself from the down-in-the-trenches parenting stuff.

I love that while you may be "mature" on the outside,

you're young on the inside.

Thanks, grandma, for loving me

unconditionally.

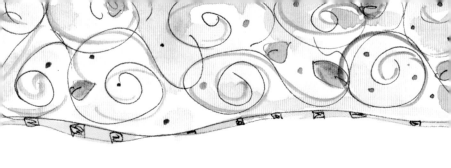

And supporting me

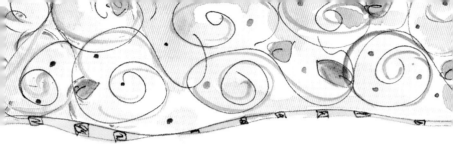

with all your heart.

You are such a
treasure in my life.

If I haven't told you lately, I want you to know

how much *I love you,* grandma.

Dear Grandma

Marianne Richmond Studios, Inc.
3900 Stinson Boulevard NE
Minneapolis, MN 55421
www.mariannerichmond.com

ISBN 10: 1-934082-54-6
ISBN 13: 978-1-934082-54-6

Illustrations by Marianne Richmond

Book design by Sara Dare Biscan

Printed in China
Second Printing
September 2009

Also available from author & illustrator
Marianne Richmond:

The Gift of an Angel
The Gift of a Memory
Hooray for You!
The Gifts of Being Grand
I Love You So...
Dear Daughter
Dear Son
Dear Granddaughter
Dear Grandson
My Shoes Take Me Where I Want to Go
Fish Kisses and Gorilla Hugs
I Love You so Much...
Happy Birthday to You!
I Wished for You, an adoption story
You are my Wish come True

To learn more about Marianne's products,
please visit
www.mariannerichmond.com